Goldendoodles Go Around the World

Colouring Book

By

Feel Happy Colouring

Want To Feel Happy?

Well you are in the right place – we are called Feel Happy Colouring Books after all!

Feel Happy Colouring are a group of talented artists that share a passion for creating fun and relaxing colouring books. We aim to help you switch off from the outside world and unleash your inner child, passion and creativity.

Please do write to us and give us your feedback, we genuinely would love to hear from you. What colouring books would you like us to do next?

Our email is help@feelhappybooks.com

We also want to post your finished artwork on our own website and Facebook page so share it with the world if you dare...

www.feelhappybooks.com

www.facebook.com/feelhappybooks

Copyright and Trademarks

This publication is Copyright © 2017 by Feel Happy Books a division of parent company, Feel Happy Limited, United Kingdom. Reg. No. 10727171

www.feelhappybooks.com

For comments, questions, requests for review copies and bulk order discounts please also email:

ISBN: 978-1-910677-22-3

Welcome to Goldendoodles Go Around the World - Volume 1

Who doesn't like Goldendoodles? Who doesn't like to travel?

It doesn't get much better than this – our lovable Goldendoodles are about to go on a vacation/holiday of a lifetime to 25 iconic destinations around the globe.

Our innovative and completely original artwork contains hand-drawn designs covering popular destinations with the last page confirming the locations our lucky Goldendoodles visited.

For multi-pet households we also have Cats Go Around the World or Dogs Go Around the World so whether you want more books to colour or ideas for gifts for friends and family we are sure to have you covered.

We have already produced specific dog breed colouring books such as the Labrador, Dachshund, French Bulldog, Poodle, Yorkie, Beagle - just let us know what we should do next.

CAN WE PLEASE ASK A SMALL FAVOUR?

Please consider helping us by 'paying it forward' – posting a positive review really does help us reach more people.

Most people don't realise this, but the more reviews we get actually helps our book get shown higher up on Amazon <u>and</u> adds more credibility for undecided buyers, so it REALLY is important for us.

Leaving comments is really simple and quick, please go to Amazon, find our book, scroll down to the bottom of the page and click where it says 'write a review.'

If you feel we can improve our books, please contact us directly as opposed to leaving permanent comments online. We are more than willing to change and improve any of our pages.

For Best Results...

1. Use this page to test your markers and pens before you start on a real picture.

2. We do recommend you put a sheet of paper or card behind each page for the ultimate protection of each page below it in case of bleed through.

3. With each picture printed on one side of the page only, it means you can remove your finished artwork and frame or display proudly without losing the picture on the other side of the page.

4. Don't feel you have to start from the first picture. Feel free to colour in any way you wish, there is no right or wrong way.

5. Reduce noise and distractions, colouring can be a great time to relax and activate your imagination.

6. Above all - have fun!

LIVINGSTONE

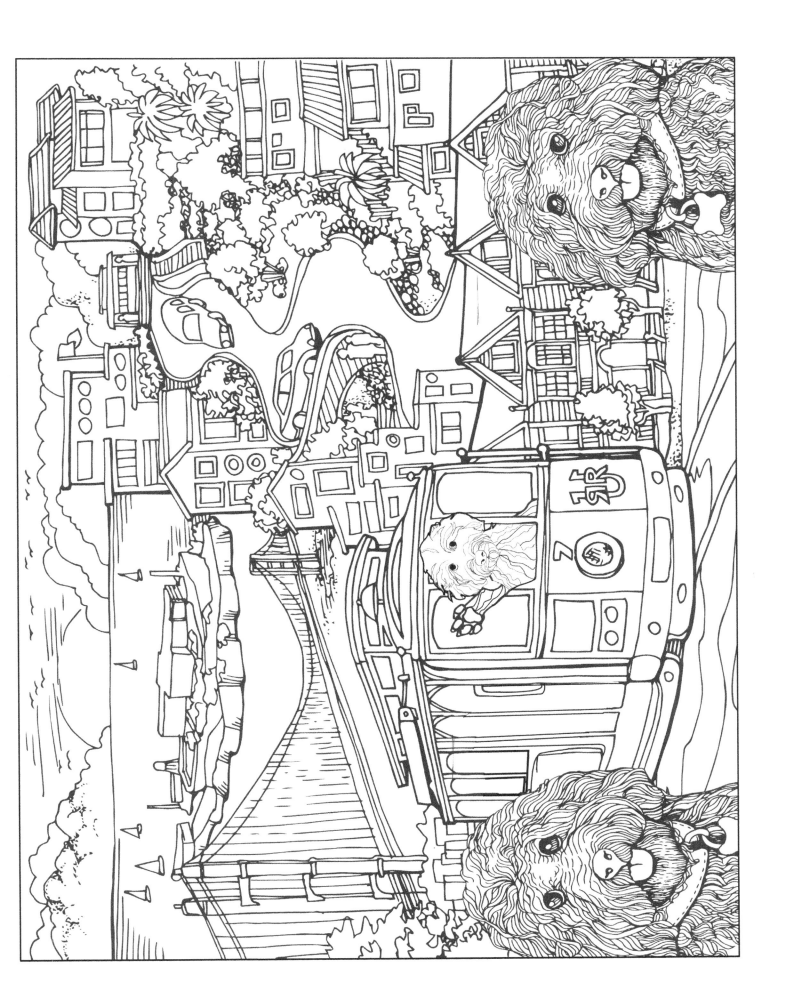

GET THE FREE BONUS EBOOK...

We want to say thank you for purchasing this book and to give you a special surprise. To show our appreciation, we have a **free e-book that you can download (and then print)** consisting of 10 sample pages from some of our other colouring books.

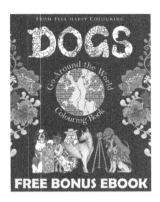

Thank you once again. To get the free book, just go to the web page below and follow the instructions. If you have any issues or feedback/comments, please send an email to help@feelhappybooks.com

www.feelhappybooks.com/secret/

We Love Amazon Reviews

Positive reviews really do help us reach more people as they help get the book shown even higher up <u>and</u> add more credibility for undecided buyers, please help us by posting a review. Go to the online retailer where you bought this book from, find our book and click on 'write a review.'

If you have any comments to help us improve the book, then we would love to hear them personally and we can then revise the book as necessary. This is far more constructive than leaving a potentially harmful review.

Thank You

We just want to say a big THANK YOU from all of us at Feel Happy Colouring for buying this book, we really do appreciate it so much.

Gift Ideas

As well as other dog colouring books we have cats too and they make great gifts for friends and family. Just search Amazon or Google for FEEL HAPPY COLOURING to find us. Here are just a small selection of our other titles…

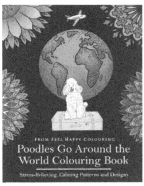

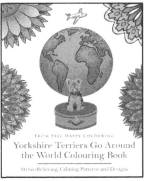

We Also Recommend…

Wouldn't it be incredible if **32 expert Goldendoodle breeders** combined with a top dog trainer to create the ultimate complete owner's guide with all your frequently asked questions answered?

Well here it is! You will literally find this book jam packed full of useful quotes giving clear advice and secret tips from the world's top Goldendoodle breeders who between them have hundreds of years of experience in caring for Goldendoodles.

This also includes two in-depth breeder interviews packed with advice and tips from **two of the founders of the Goldendoodle Association of North America (GANA).**

President Amy Lane says: "This book will be your go to for all questions related to Goldendoodles. It will assist you in your search for the right breeder all the way through caring for your dog in his/her senior years. It is packed full of information directly from the expert breeders of Goldendoodles. There are a lot of "Goldendoodle" books, but if you must buy just one, this is it!"

On sale at all good online book stores including Amazon.

Made in the USA
Coppell, TX
21 January 2023

11460042R00037